Pandemic Strategies and the Global Economy

Ellen Rodger

CRABTREE PUBLISHING COMPANY
WWW.CRABTREEBOOKS.COM

Author:
Ellen Rodger

Series research and development:
Janine Deschenes and Ellen Rodger

Editorial director:
Kathy Middleton

Editor:
Janine Deschenes

Proofreader:
Wendy Scavuzzo

Graphic design:
Samara Parent

Image research:
Samara Parent

Print coordinator:
Katherine Berti

Images:
Alamy
 Jeremy Pembrey: p. 6 (bottom)
 Cynthia Lee: p. 6-7 (top)
 SOPA Images Limited: p. 11
 REUTERS: p. 12-13 (top);
  p. 17 (bottom right)
 Kirn Vintage Stock: p. 14
 Robert Wallace / Wallace Media
  Network: p. 24
 Ron Adar: p. 25
 GL Archive: p. 28 (bottom left)
 Science History Images: p. 28 (bottom right)
 PA Images: p. 33 (bottom)
 White House Photo: p. 38
 Newscom: p. 40

The Canadian Press
 Graham Hughes: p. 39

Library of Congress
 LC-DIG-matpc-00822: p. 31

Shutterstock
 Sk Hasan Ali: front cover (top right)
 Nor Sham Soyod: p. 3
 Ricky kuo: p. 4-5
 Igor Corovic: p. 8
 JL Images: p. 10 (top)
 faboi: p. 12 (bottom); p. 16-17 (top)
 Marcus Krauss: p. 15 (bottom)
 Caio Pederneiras: p. 18-19 (top)
 michelmond: p. 18 (bottom)
 TZIDO SUN: p. 20-21 (top)
 Jennifer M. Mason: p. 22
 Yuri Turkov: p. 23 (bottom)
 ThreeEyedRavenProductions: p. 27
 Loveandrock: p. 29
 Philip Pilosian: p. 33 (top)
 Richard Stephen: p. 34
 Olga Mukashev: p. 36
 Ron Adar: p. 36-37 (top)
 Micha Serraf: p. 41
 kandl stock: p. 45

Wikimedia Commons
 Krdobyns and Innisfree987: p. 15 (top)

All other images by Shutterstock

Library and Archives Canada Cataloguing in Publication

Title: Pandemic strategies and the global economy / Ellen Rodger.
Names: Rodger, Ellen, author.
Description: Series statement: COVID-19: meeting the challenge | Includes bibliographical references and index.
Identifiers: Canadiana (print) 20210214732 | Canadiana (ebook) 20210214740 | ISBN 9781427156099 (hardcover) | ISBN 9781427156112 (softcover) | ISBN 9781427156136 (HTML) | ISBN 9781427156457 (EPUB)
Subjects: LCSH: COVID-19 (Disease)—Juvenile literature. | LCSH: COVID-19 (Disease)—Government policy—Juvenile literature. | LCSH: COVID-19 Pandemic, 2020—Social aspects—Juvenile literature. | LCSH: COVID-19 Pandemic, 2020-—Economic aspects—Juvenile literature. | LCSH: Epidemics—Prevention—Juvenile literature.
Classification: LCC RA644.C67 R63 2022 | DDC j616.2/414--dc23

Library of Congress Cataloging-in-Publication Data

Names: Rodger, Ellen, author.
Title: Pandemic strategies and the global economy / Ellen Rodger.
Description: New York, NY : Crabtree Publishing Company, [2022] | Series: COVID-19: meeting the challenge | Includes bibliographical references and index.
Identifiers: LCCN 2021020771 (print) | LCCN 2021020772 (ebook) | ISBN 9781427156099 (hardcover) | ISBN 9781427156112 (paperback) | ISBN 9781427156136 (ebook) | ISBN 9781427156457 (epub)
Subjects: LCSH: COVID-19 (Disease)--Economic aspects. | COVID-19 (Disease)--Government policy.
Classification: LCC RA644.C67 R63 2022 (print) | LCC RA644.C67 (ebook) | DDC 362.1962/414--dc23
LC record available at https://lccn.loc.gov/2021020771
LC ebook record available at https://lccn.loc.gov/2021020772

Crabtree Publishing Company

www.crabtreebooks.com 1-800-387-7650

Copyright © **2022 CRABTREE PUBLISHING COMPANY.**
All rights reserved. No part of this publication may be reproduced, stored in a retrieval system or be transmitted in any form or by any means, electronic, mechanical, photocopying, recording, or otherwise, without the prior written permission of Crabtree Publishing Company. In Canada: We acknowledge the financial support of the Government of Canada through the Canada Book Fund for our publishing activities.

Published in Canada
Crabtree Publishing
616 Welland Ave.
St. Catharines, Ontario
L2M 5V6

Published in the United States
Crabtree Publishing
347 Fifth Ave
Suite 1402-145
New York, NY 10016

Printed in the U.S.A./092021/CG20210616

CONTENTS

Introduction 4

Chapter 1
A New Virus 6

Chapter 2
Swift Science 12

Chapter 3
The Battle
for Lives 20

Chapter 4
Government
Responses 34

Chapter 5
Preparing for
the Future 40

Bibliography 44

Timeline 45

Learning More 46

Glossary 46

Index 48

About the Author 48

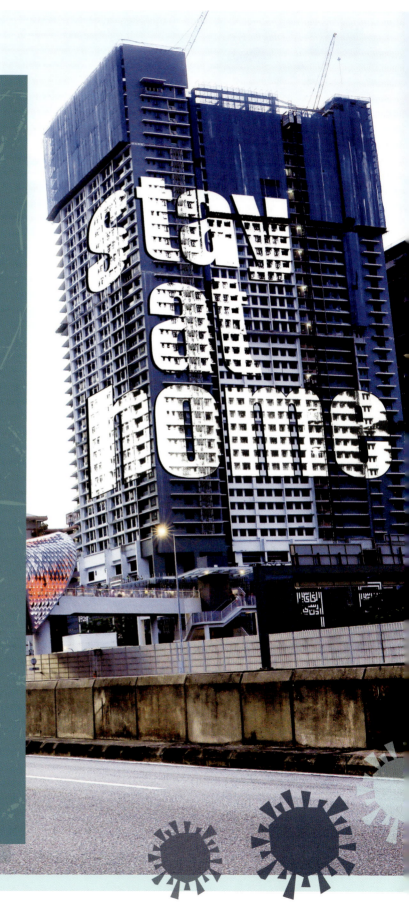

Introduction

At first, it was just a rumor online and in social media. An unknown virus was attacking people's lungs and making it difficult for them to breathe.

The rumor said hospitals in the Chinese city of Wuhan were preparing for a major outbreak. Even before China officially confirmed it had a serious problem, the government in the nearby island country of Taiwan swung into action. Just 180 miles (130 km) of ocean separate Taiwan from China. Many people travel between the two countries. Taiwan quickly began **screening** travelers coming from Wuhan, looking for the virus. On December 21, 2019, the country's Central **Epidemic** Command Center started organizing and buying supplies of masks and **personal protective equipment** (PPE) to help keep people from becoming ill.

By the time scientists officially named the mysterious disease COVID-19 on February 11, 2020, Taiwan was already following plans aimed at stopping the virus from spreading. They included preventing non-Taiwanese from entering the country without special permits, quickly testing people, **isolating** them, and **tracing** their contacts. COVID-19 wasn't Taiwan's first experience with a hard-hitting worldwide disease, or pandemic. In 2003, the **SARS pandemic** killed 181 people in Taiwan. The SARS experience was a hard lesson. This time, the country was more prepared. A plan to save lives was rolled out.

For the next 255 days, Taiwan recorded zero cases of COVID-19 within the local population. Life went on almost as before and the country's **economy** remained strong. At the same time, many other countries had hundreds and, later thousands of COVID-19 deaths per day. In those countries, many jobs were lost and businesses suffered—some closing forever.

Taiwan has a population of almost 24 million people in a small country. It recorded 770 COVID-19 cases from January to December 2020. A rise in cases in May 2021 was linked to people not being careful.

In April 2020, a Taiwan hotel spells "zero 5" with room lights. It marked zero cases of COVID-19 for five straight days in the country. Taiwan became an example of good government pandemic strategies. Strategies are plans of action designed to achieve specific aims, such as saving lives and supporting the economy.

Chapter 1

A New Virus

With 11-million people, Wuhan is one of China's most heavily populated cities. When hospitals began to fill up with very sick people in January 2020, government officials learned they had a serious problem. How would they keep a mysterious new virus from spreading to more people?

At first, China's government denied the new disease was a threat. It tried to stop doctors and journalists from speaking out about the growing number of patients with the same symptoms. Before the virus even had a name, Wuhan eye doctor Li Wenliang sent a message to fellow doctors on December 30, telling them he was worried about a rapidly-spreading disease. He was accused of spreading rumors and the Chinese government officials warned him to stop. But it could not ignore the numbers of sick people. By late January, the government had to admit it had an outbreak on its hands.

China tested 9 million people for COVID-19 within a few weeks. One scientific study estimated all the health measures China took from January 29 to February 29, 2020, prevented 1.4 million infections and 56,000 deaths.

Dr. Li Wenliang was considered a hero by many for sounding the alarm. He became ill with COVID-19 after treating a woman with an eye disease. He did not know she had been infected with COVID-19. He died of the disease on February 6, 2020.

China built 16 field hospitals in public stadiums and exhibition halls in January and February 2020. These were used to isolate COVID-19 patients instead of keeping them at home where they might infect other family members. By March, the hospitals were no longer needed.

China's Lockdown

Once China acknowledged the virus, it took strong measures to control its spread and study it. Wuhan and 15 other cities in the same Chinese province of Hubei were put on a strict **lockdown** on January 23. Trains, flights, and roads were blocked. Almost 760 million people were told to stay at home. **Field hospitals** were built quickly to help with an expected overflow of patients from city hospitals.

The lockdown proved effective in slowing the **transmission** of the virus and saving lives. By April 2020, new infections in China dwindled to a trickle. The Chinese government then ended its 76-day lockdown of Wuhan and many other Chinese cities.

Gearing Up

China did more than try to control the virus spread. On January 10, 2020, Chinese scientists sequenced, or determined the structure of the virus's genome. Genomes are genetic materials, or the information all living things pass on from one generation to the next. The sequencing was completed a month before the **World Health Organization (WHO)** officially named the virus severe acute **respiratory** syndrome coronavirus 2 (SARS-CoV-2).

The disease caused by this virus was called COVID-19. Sequencing the virus helped scientists all over the world study how this disease evolved from an animal virus to a human virus. It also helped pinpoint where the virus likely came from: a Wuhan seafood market that sold exotic animals for food.

Chapter 1

Each country has its own ways of preparing for and managing threatening diseases. Some close country borders to outside travelers. Australia brought in border restrictions between states within the country to slow the spread of COVID-19. Here cars line up at a checkpoint in the state of Queensland. Restrictions loosened as the spread of COVID-19 lessened.

Spread Throughout the World

Most of the world was also slow to respond to COVID-19. The virus and disease spread outside of China—carried by travelers who went all over the world. The virus was "novel," or new to humans. This meant there was no **immunity** and every human on Earth was at risk of contracting it. It spread easily, by respiratory droplets exhaled by coughing or talking. Often, people infected by the virus showed no symptoms of the COVID-19 disease. These people were asymptomatic. This meant they could easily and unknowingly spread the virus. Scientists believe the virus was spreading throughout the world for weeks before it was officially recognized.

Public Health Emergency

Governments throughout the world watched nervously. The WHO also monitored the spread of the virus. On January 30, 2020, confirmed cases reached 7,818 in a total of 19 countries. The WHO then declared a **Public Health** Emergency of International Concern. This was the WHO's warning that the virus and disease were risks to people in countries throughout the world. The declaration was intended to alert countries to prepare their people and economies for what was coming.

One year after the virus emerged, confirmed cases of COVID-19 reached more than 110 million worldwide, with deaths at 2.4 million and counting. Scientists believe the number of infections was greater, as many people had mild symptoms and were not tested.

A NEW VIRUS

Pandemic Status

On March 11, 2020, as the number of people getting very sick and dying from COVID-19 ballooned, the WHO declared COVID-19 a pandemic. Pandemics are disease outbreaks that are widespread and often worldwide. They affect a large number of people. COVID-19 was the first pandemic declared since 2009–2010, when the **H1N1** virus spread across the world. That virus killed an estimated 100,000 to 400,000 people worldwide in its first year. No country wanted to risk the lives of its people again. But not all had the ability to limit the spread of the virus, and none knew exactly how dangerous COVID-19 would be.

Long after the virus became a pandemic, the exact beginnings of COVID-19 remained mysterious. Researchers knew it came out of China and hopped from an animal host, such as a bat, to a human host.

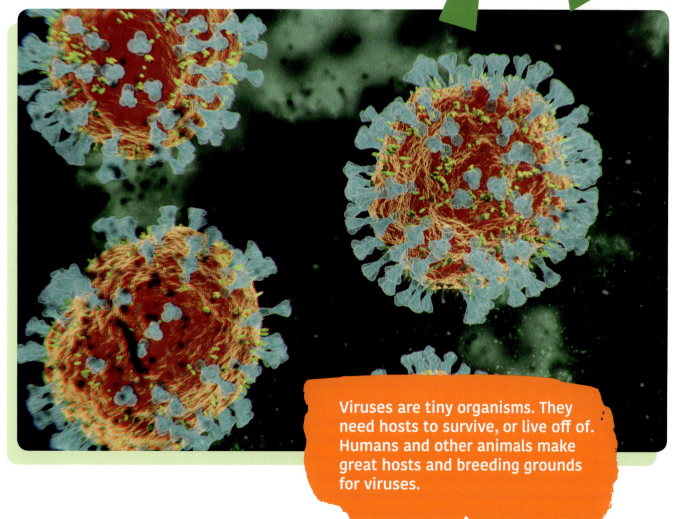

Viruses are tiny organisms. They need hosts to survive, or live off of. Humans and other animals make great hosts and breeding grounds for viruses.

Chapter 1

Border closings during COVID-19 restricted travelers in many countries. Trucks carrying food and other essential goods were allowed to cross.

Learning Curve

The world has had several pandemics over the past 100 years. Each pandemic is a lesson in protection and prevention. In the 1918 to 1920 flu pandemic, there were few ways to help people survive. Drugs that stopped viruses from making people very ill had not yet been invented. Hospital care was basic. Many sick people didn't even make it to hospitals. They died at home. Back then, preventing infection from occurring was the most important thing. Some early methods used to prevent infections were keeping the sick isolated, washing hands, and wearing masks. These were not 100 percent effective, but they did help. They became the same basic protection steps public health officials urged people to use in 2020 to 2021.

World on Edge

COVID-19 made the world stop and take notice. Not every country responded to the virus's threat in the same way. Dozens of countries ordered some form of lockdown early in the pandemic. Many of these lockdowns were not as strict as those imposed by the government in Wuhan, China. The purpose of lockdowns was to prevent the virus from spreading throughout communities.

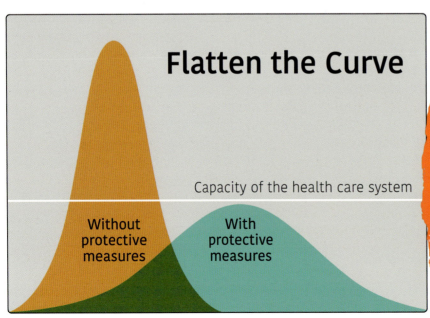

Public health officials stated the lockdowns were key to "flattening the curve," or lowering the numbers of people testing positive at the same time. A sharp rise would make it difficult for hospitals to cope with the number of sick people.

10

PANDEMIC HEROES

Zhang Zhan, Citizen Journalist

As hospitals in Wuhan were filling with COVID-19 patients in early February 2020, several Chinese citizen journalists traveled there to get the news out. Zhang Zhan was one of them. Citizen journalists are people who don't work for regular newspapers or media outlets. They still gather information, make sure it is truthful, and share it with the world. China is a **Communist** country that controls its media. It also controls what information ordinary people can share and how they can share it. A former lawyer, Zhang Zhan's live online reports on hospitals overflowing with COVID-19 patients embarrassed the government. She was seen as a threat. Zhang went missing on May 14. On December 28, 2020, she was sentenced to four years in jail. Her crime was officially "picking **quarrels** and **provoking** trouble."

Citizen journalists provide information that China's official media will not print or broadcast. Here, activists in Hong Kong demand that the government free 12 local activists and Zhang Zhan.

Chapter 2
Swift Science

The scientific response to COVID-19 was blindingly fast. For decades, infectious disease experts had said the world would likely experience another major pandemic. They just didn't know the month or the year. When it seemed COVID-19 was that pandemic, scientists got right to work. Many years of research were compressed into one year.

It takes a few weeks after a vaccine is administered for the body to build immunity to a disease. That's why even after a shot, a vaccinated person has to be careful. It is possible for a person to be infected just before or just after vaccination because the vaccine didn't have enough time to build protection.

Medical Milestones

Scientists around the world worked in different labs. They shared important information to help make effective treatments and vaccines for COVID-19. Normally, it takes years to develop a vaccine for a disease. But scientists had two head starts on COVID-19. One was the decades of research already done on coronaviruses. Another was the quick sequencing Chinese researchers had done and released to the world on SARS-CoV-2.

Coronaviruses are a group of viruses with a specific **genetic structure**. The respiratory diseases SARS and MERS (Middle East respiratory syndrome) are also caused by coronaviruses. Scientists had been working on new types of vaccines for them for many years. That science was used to help create the first COVID-19 vaccines.

Some vaccines require one shot. Others require more. The first COVID-19 vaccines required two. Here medical workers in Italy give vaccines to people in a school gym.

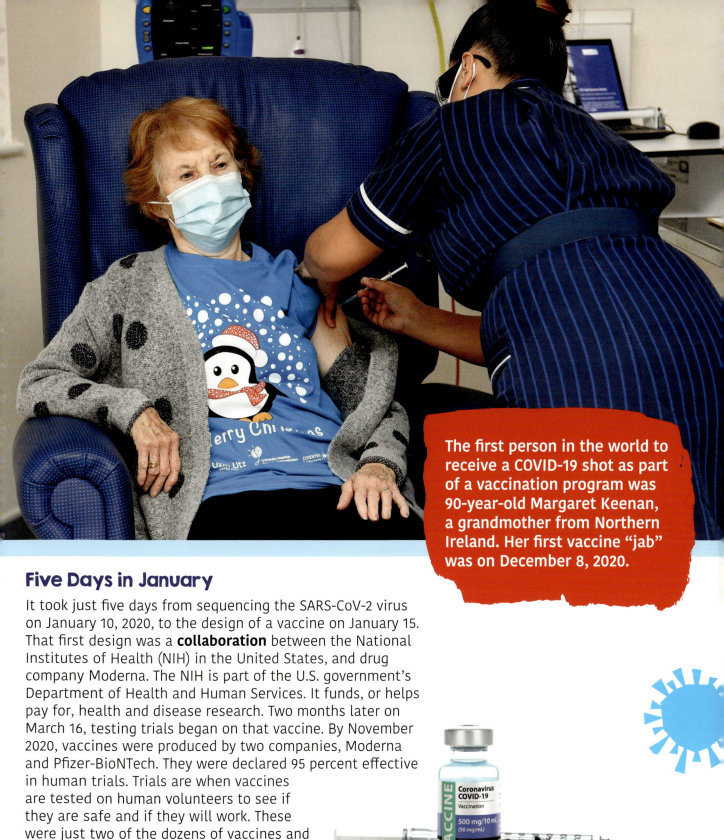

The first person in the world to receive a COVID-19 shot as part of a vaccination program was 90-year-old Margaret Keenan, a grandmother from Northern Ireland. Her first vaccine "jab" was on December 8, 2020.

Five Days in January

It took just five days from sequencing the SARS-CoV-2 virus on January 10, 2020, to the design of a vaccine on January 15. That first design was a **collaboration** between the National Institutes of Health (NIH) in the United States, and drug company Moderna. The NIH is part of the U.S. government's Department of Health and Human Services. It funds, or helps pay for, health and disease research. Two months later on March 16, testing trials began on that vaccine. By November 2020, vaccines were produced by two companies, Moderna and Pfizer-BioNTech. They were declared 95 percent effective in human trials. Trials are when vaccines are tested on human volunteers to see if they are safe and if they will work. These were just two of the dozens of vaccines and thousands of drug treatments designed to fight COVID-19. Teams of researchers and drug companies were working on these all over the world.

Chapter 2

Rapid Response

The race to find treatments and vaccines for COVID-19 was one of the most urgent health challenges in modern times. Medical researchers never know if or when they will find a "cure" for a disease. That means new treatments and vaccines are always in the works. A new, fast-spreading disease that is threatening the entire world will have more researchers working on it and more funding from governments and other organizations. This was the case with COVID-19.

First Vaccines

The first two COVID-19 vaccines were called messenger ribonucleic acid, or mRNA vaccines. They were based on 40 years of research on the **hereditary** material in humans and almost all other life forms. It normally takes many years to create a new vaccine. The decades of research on mRNA made it possible to produce the fastest vaccine on record. It went into human arms within 10 months instead of 10 years. mRNA carries information that is necessary for a body to work as it should. The mRNA vaccines are unlike other vaccines. They give sets of instructions to the body's **cells** to make **proteins** that prevent or fight disease. Most traditional vaccines are made from killed or weakened viruses, which encourage the body to build an immune response to the disease.

The previous record for quick vaccine production was made with the mumps vaccine. It was developed in four years and first used in 1963. Mumps is a contagious, or easily spread, disease that is caused by a virus. It can be very serious and lead to brain infections, hearing loss, and heart problems.

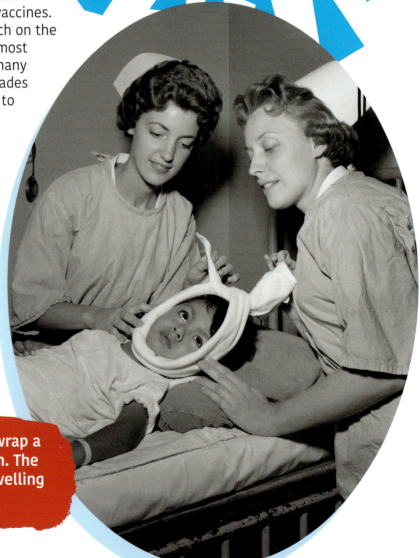

In the 1960s, two nurses wrap a cloth around a child's chin. The tight cloth helped with swelling caused by the mumps.

SWIFT SCIENCE

PANDEMIC WHO'S WHO

Dr. Katalin Karikó

Fellow scientists have credited the work done by **biochemist** Dr. Katalin Karikó as the reason why the first COVID-19 vaccines were produced so quickly. The Hungarian-born scientist spent her entire career researching mRNA. She believed it was a key to finding treatments and cures for dozens of diseases and health conditions.

For most of her career, Dr. Karikó's work was underappreciated. She had to fight for a portion of the money given to researchers by universities and governments. She often got no funding at all. Dr. Karikó was also denied higher-paying jobs at the university where she worked because her research wasn't flashy and didn't bring immediate results. But Dr. Karikó's determination wasn't dimmed. She continued her work and experiments. In the early 2000s, she teamed with research partner Dr. Drew Weissman. The pair quietly determined how synthetic, or human-made, mRNA could be changed to work inside the body's cells. They also found a way to deliver it so that the body's natural defenses would not reject it. Years later, these breakthroughs would be the building blocks of the first COVID-19 vaccines made by Pfizer-BioNTech and Moderna.

The vaccines developed with Dr. Karikó's work use mRNA to deliver a coded message to the human body when they are injected. The body then triggers an immune response.

Dr. Karikó was also hired by BioNTech. Her work and knowledge may be used to develop treatments for many other diseases.

Chapter 2

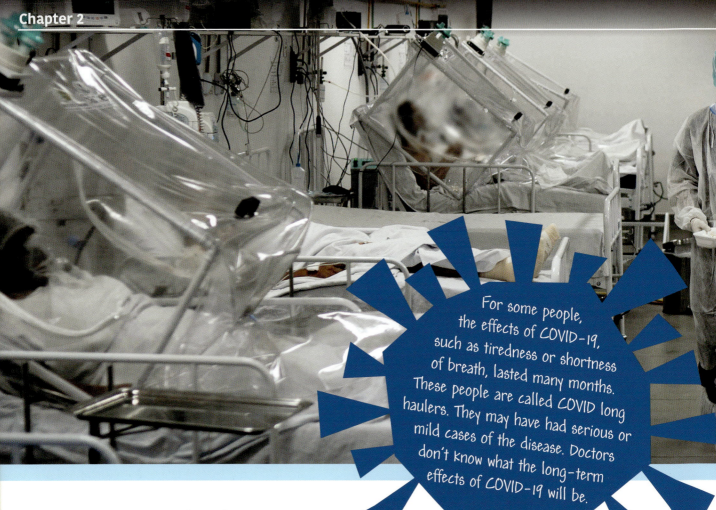

For some people, the effects of COVID-19, such as tiredness or shortness of breath, lasted many months. These people are called COVID long haulers. They may have had serious or mild cases of the disease. Doctors don't know what the long-term effects of COVID-19 will be.

Treatments on the Fly

COVID-19's rapid spread led medical professionals to use everything in their toolboxes to help people stay alive. In hospitals, a **battlefield medicine** mentality took over. Doctors made quick **innovations** in how patients with COVID-19 were treated.

Early Treatments

During the **first wave** of the pandemic, doctors were just learning how the virus affected the body. They often tried different treatments to keep people alive. At first, they put sick patients on ventilators early. Ventilators are machines with tubes that go down the mouth and into the windpipe. They help people breathe when they can't do it on their own. Ventilators were used to help patients survive and get better. Doctors also used strong sedatives, or drugs that helped patients rest.

Developing New Methods

Within weeks of dealing with very ill patients, doctors were abandoning treatments that did not seem to work. They also developed new ways of caring for patients, and shared them with other doctors around the world. By the time the **second wave** hit, doctors and nurses were checking patients more often and using ventilators only when absolutely needed. New drugs were tried. Some prevented organs such as the heart and kidneys from failing. Others helped keep people with milder symptoms from becoming seriously ill.

SWIFT SCIENCE

About five percent of people who contracted the virus became seriously ill, or sick enough to be in hospital.

Tailoring Treatment

Intensive care units are where the sickest people were treated. There, medical staff placed many COVID-19 patients on their stomachs to help their breathing. This technique is called the prone position. It was used a lot because it helped patients get more oxygen in their blood and more easily to their lungs. The effectiveness of the prone position was published in a **medical journal** less than a decade before COVID-19. Hospitals tailored, or adapted, the technique during COVID-19. It was used on patients who were on ventilators, and patients who were not.

A nurse tends to a COVID-19 patient in a prone position.

Ventilator Innovation

Respiratory therapists (RTs) or nurses remove patients from ventilators once they are healthy enough to breathe on their own. They also remove them when people die. Removing tubes from patients is a difficult process. There is a danger of spreading the virus as patients cough or let out air from the lungs. During the first wave of COVID-19, RTs developed a safer way of taking patients off ventilators. It involved placing a large plastic bag over a patient to "capture" any particles from the lungs. This innovation created less viral spread and reduced the chances of infecting medical staff.

17

Chapter 2

Learning How to Cope

In some countries, hospitals were overwhelmed by the number of people sick with COVID-19. Patients were cared for in hospital hallways, or sometimes even in parking lots. Some countries used their militaries to help out. In spring 2020, the U.S. government sent a hospital ship to help care for COVID-19 overflow patients in New York City. Military doctors and support staff were also sent to several other states to help with patients. China is believed to have prepared 10,000 troops for COVID-19 support duties.

Healers Getting Sick

The sick weren't the only people battling COVID-19. Hospital and health care workers all over the world risked their lives to help. In the first wave particularly, many workers did not have enough personal protective equipment (PPE) to keep them safe. Some had to wear the same masks for days. This contributed to them contracting the highly-infectious disease on the job.

From January to August 2020, 1,500 nurses across the globe had died of COVID-19. By April 2020, only four months into the pandemic, 150 doctors in Italy had died after contracting COVID-19 from patients. Italy, like the UK, Spain, and the state of New York, suffered badly during the first wave of the pandemic.

Tricky Virus

The SARS-CoV-2 coronavirus is tricky. It spread easily throughout the world. It also mutated, or changed over time, into several different variants, or versions. Not all of these variants made the COVID-19 disease more severe, but they did make it easier to transmit. This meant people around the world were even more in danger of contracting the virus.

COVID-19 testing determined the number of cases in an area and allowed governments and hospitals to prepare. Mass testing was sometimes carried out in parking lots.

SWIFT SCIENCE

In many countries, mobile hospitals, such as those used during wars, were set up in fields and parking lots. These took the pressure off of hospitals and allowed COVID-19 patients to be isolated better from other patients.

Virus Variants

Scientists know that viruses mutate to better survive. They warned that most of the world would need to be vaccinated before everyone was considered safe from COVID-19. The longer a virus is out passing from person to person, the more mutations there will be. There is also a greater chance that a vaccine will not work well against one of the mutations. Researchers moved quickly to study the COVID-19 variants. They wanted to see whether drug treatments and vaccines would be effective against them. Vaccine makers set to work on booster shots that work against the main new virus variants. These shots would provide added protection against some variants.

There are many COVID-19 variants. In June 2021, the WHO renamed the main ones Alpha, Beta, Gamma, and Delta, after letters in the Greek alphabet. The WHO wanted to remove the stigma caused by naming them for the places they were discovered.

19

Chapter 3
The Battle for Lives

Wash your hands, keep your distance, stay at home. By March 2020, these phrases had almost become a chant. They were used to educate people on the basic measures used to prevent catching COVID-19. And the biggest and loudest chanters around the world were public health experts.

Disease Warriors

Public health is a government service that focuses on all the things that keep a population safe and healthy. These things include research, educating people about healthy living, and providing advice about diseases. When it was clear that COVID-19 was a threat to lives around the world, public health took the lead. Public health experts were the people who spoke at **press conferences**. They updated the public on what was known about the new disease. They gave governments advice on how to reduce the threat of the virus and save lives. But it was up to governments—and citizens—to follow that advice.

Public health officials say masks should cover the nose and mouth.

20

When evidence showed wearing masks could help prevent transmission of the virus, public health officials advised people to wear them.

Knowledge of COVID-19 changed over time as scientists and doctors learned more about it. Public health explained the complicated science for everyone.

Chapter 3

People line up outside a grocery store following public health advice to keep a safe distance of at least six feet (2 m) from each other.

In the United States, the Centers for Disease Control and Prevention (CDC) is the country's leading public health **agency**. In Canada, that role is taken on by the Public Health Agency of Canada. Different states, provinces, and cities also have public health agencies and departments. They all work to develop plans and practices on how to keep people safe from diseases.

Science Fights Speculation

Public health experts continually updated information on how COVID-19 spread and what were the **best practices** for avoiding infection. Those practices changed over time. In the beginning, for example, most experts felt it wasn't necessary for ordinary people to wear a mask. Later, when they learned more about the disease and how it spread, public health experts began advising people to wear two masks in public places where they could not keep a safe distance from others. More research led to better advice on keeping people safe. Early in the pandemic, shoppers were advised to scrub their groceries down with detergent and water. This would kill any virus particles that may have landed on food. That advice changed when research showed there was no evidence that food packaging spread the virus.

THE BATTLE FOR LIVES

Quarantine is a health practice used to keep people who have COVID-19 away from others to prevent spread of the disease. Hospitals quarantined COVID-19 patients in special areas.

PANDEMIC WHO'S WHO

Maria DeJoseph Van Kerkhove

You might have seen Dr. Maria DeJoseph Van Kerkhove talking about COVID research at World Health Organization (WHO) press conferences. Confident and clear, she was described as a "disease detective." She wrote hundreds of advice papers on COVID-19. An American **epidemiologist**, Dr. Van Kerkhove is a specialist in emerging infectious diseases. These are diseases, like COVID-19, that are new to humans. She coordinated the WHO's COVID "response" team. In February 2020, Dr. Van Kerkhove spent two weeks in China as part of a team gathering information about the COVID-19 outbreak and how China was fighting it. When she returned to her home in Geneva, Switzerland, some team members tested positive. Her knowledge of infectious diseases told her that quarantine was the best way to keep others safe. So, she self-quarantined to be sure she would not spread any virus to her family. That meant two months of not touching her two children and only talking to them through windows at their home. She also advised people early on, in February 2020, that the "new normal" for the pandemic would be physical distancing. She cautioned that people would not be able to be with friends and loved ones for long periods of time.

Dr. Van Kerkhove works at the WHO's office in Geneva.

Chapter 3

Some people thought that because the COVID-19 vaccines were developed so quickly, they must therefore be unsafe. Scientists point to the fact the science behind the vaccines was 40 years in the making. All vaccines and drugs involve some risk, but vaccine-makers also follow testing guidelines.

Fighting Falsehoods

Some scientists believed there were two pandemics with COVID-19. One was the real disease pandemic, and the other a worldwide outbreak of lies and misinformation about COVID-19. They called this an infodemic. They believe the lies and misinformation cost lives because they convinced some people that COVID-19 posed little or no danger. These people then did not follow basic advice from government public health experts on how to protect themselves and others, such as maintaining distance and wearing masks.

Social Media and the Pandemic

A study by researchers at Harvard University in Boston, Massachusetts, found that social media contributed to many people not believing scientists and doctors. Some articles shared on social media were designed to make people distrust science, doctors, and governments. They also encouraged people to believe that COVID-19 was a hoax, that it was no more dangerous than the flu, and that vaccines were unsafe. This anti-science **bias** and distrust was further fueled by some media outlets.

THE BATTLE FOR LIVES

Fighting Stigma

Governments and health agencies began public education campaigns to fight misinformation. In the U.S., the Centers for Disease Control (CDC) cautioned people not to form ideas about COVID-19 too early. In Canada, the Centre for Addiction and Mental Health (CAMH) advised people to read credible sources for COVID-19 information. Credible sources include news outlets with trained journalists and reputations for checking facts. It also noted that there was a rise in stigma about people who got COVID-19. Stigma is negative beliefs and **stereotypes** about someone or something. There was also an increase in stigma against people of Chinese or Asian **ethnicity**. This is because the virus emerged in China. The CDC and CAMH also advised people not to use the terms "China virus" or "Wuhan flu." These terms encouraged people to **discriminate** against people of Asian ethnicities.

Pandemic Mental Health

With normal routines sent topsy-turvy by the pandemic, people's mental health suffered. Studies showed 4 in 10 adults in the U.S. suffered symptoms of anxiety or depression. Young adults were particularly affected. Fifty-six percent of 18 to 24-year-olds in one poll reported heightened symptoms of depression. Drug use also increased as more people were isolated from others.

From January 2020 to September 2020, scientists published more than 23,600 papers on the virus. Some were studies that showed how well drug treatments worked. Others were on how health care workers' mental health suffered because they were caring for so many sick and dying patients.

Governments worried that people's fear about COVID-19 would influence them to want to blame someone. This could cause rumors and myths to spread, leading to acts of hate.

Chapter 3

Drug Overdoses

The CDC called drug overdoses and deaths in the United States an epidemic of its own. From May 2019 to May 2, 2020, more than 81,000 Americans died of drug overdoses. It was the highest number of overdose deaths ever recorded in the country in a 12-month period. Five of those months were during the pandemic. The **statistics** showed overdose deaths increased the most during the pandemic.

The Canadian province of British Columbia also had record deaths due to drug overdoses in 2020. An average 4.7 people died per day of overdoses in 2020. This was up from 2.7 deaths per day in 2019. This led the province to ask the government of Canada to make new laws to help prevent future overdoses.

Disruption of Routines

Experts believe the higher number of deaths was due to people using more drugs to help with stress during the pandemic. The pandemic also interrupted counseling and treatment programs for people coping with drug addictions. This led many people to start using drugs again.

There was already a drug overdose problem before COVID-19. It was made worse by COVID-19 safety regulations such as social distancing. There were also more pressures on health care systems due to more COVID patients.

Violence and Abuse

Pandemic experts and governments urged people to stay safe at home during the pandemic. However, some people's homes became even less safe. Studies showed intimate partner violence (IPV) increased as pandemic stress increased. Intimate partner violence is abuse that occurs between domestic partners and spouses. Normally, one in four women and one in ten men experience IPV. In March 2020, U.S. police departments reported increases as high as 27 percent in family violence calls.

One New England Journal of Medicine paper noted that the number of calls to IPV hotlines dropped by 50 percent. Many victims sheltering with their abusers had no way to safely ask for help. Their partners, at home full time, were constantly watching and controlling them. In Canada, a national survey showed 82 percent of gender-based violence (GBV) shelter workers noticed that during COVID-19, people experienced a higher severity of violence. GBV is violence against someone because of their gender. Shelters also had to follow COVID-19 distancing and safety rules. This meant they could not accept as many people.

Chapter 3

Containing the Virus

Governments all over the world used different measures to control the spread of the virus. Many of those measures were last used during times of great emergency, such as war. Most governments understood that if no effort was made to contain the virus, it would spread widely. Hundreds of millions of people could be infected, causing widespread death.

Previous Pandemic Lessons

It is thought that 500 million people worldwide were infected during the 1918 to 1920 flu pandemic. It is also known as the Spanish flu pandemic. An estimated 50 million people died. That pandemic came in waves and lasted three years. One thing researchers learned about that pandemic was that governments need to coordinate efforts to control how disease spreads. They also need to communicate better with citizens when there is a disease threat. Researchers also learned that containing a virus early on saves lives.

To decide what containment measures to take, governments used the R number. This is the number of people that one infected person will pass the virus on to. The higher the R number, the greater the spread and the stricter the government's control measures.

The origin of the 1918 to 1920 pandemic is unknown. It was called the Spanish flu because Spain was one of the first countries to report it. From studying it, scientists now know it did not start there. By the time it ended, one-third of the world had been infected.

THE BATTLE FOR LIVES

Monitoring and Lockdowns

More than 150 governments around the world used some sort of monitoring and lockdown plan to slow the spread of COVID-19. Monitoring meant watching the number of confirmed cases. It also meant setting rules for behavior, such as mandatory mask-wearing in public buildings. Lockdowns were designed to control the movement of people. By doing that, the movement of the virus could be controlled.

Governments had different levels of monitoring and lockdown plans. They were measured in numbers or colors. For example, the Canadian province of Ontario had a color system with five levels. The first level was green, or "prevent." It was the level used when numbers of confirmed COVID-19 infections were lowest. The levels continued with yellow for protect, orange for restrict, red for control, and gray for lockdown. The government also used stay-at home orders when cases surged.

Lockdown Rules

The rules for strict lockdowns varied. Generally, schools and businesses were shut and people ordered to stay at home for many weeks or months. In some places, curfews that began at 8 p.m., were ordered. People caught breaking them were given fines by police. In some places, however, there were no lockdowns at all and schools and businesses remained open.

> Lockdowns helped lower the number of cases so hospitals were not overflowing with sick people. Many places such as London, England, experienced a series of repeated lockdowns.

Chapter 3

Disease Inequality

During the early days of the pandemic, government officials often said "we are all in this together." This statement was intended to stress how one person's actions—such as not wearing a mask or social distancing—can affect everyone. But COVID-19 proved that diseases don't affect populations equally. Some groups suffered more than others.

Age, Race, and Class

COVID-19 didn't create inequalities between people throughout the world. But it did make them more visible. It showed how poverty, age, race, and poor health made some more at risk of serious illness and death from COVID-19. According to the **World Economic Forum (WEF)**, Black Americans were almost twice as likely to live in areas more affected by COVID-19. Black, Indigenous, Hispanic, and Latinx populations recorded more deaths per 100,000 people in the United States during the first wave of COVID-19. In Canada, the elderly in care homes were most at risk during the first wave.

Some people worked long hours in jobs that put them at more risk, but were not paid for sick leave. Others were more at risk because they lived in overcrowded housing where isolating is impossible.

THE BATTLE FOR LIVES

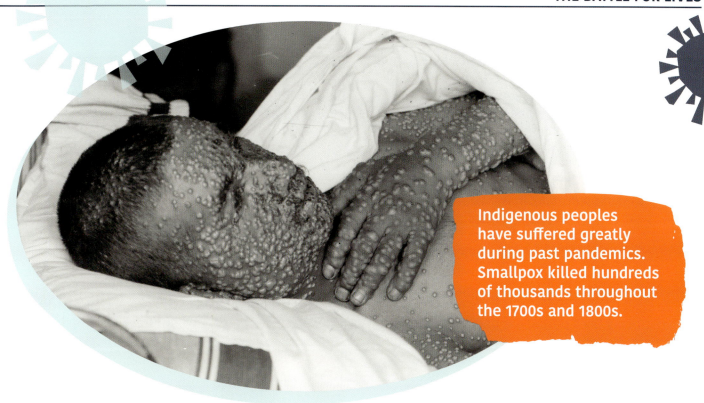

Indigenous peoples have suffered greatly during past pandemics. Smallpox killed hundreds of thousands throughout the 1700s and 1800s.

Indigenous Populations

The United Nations noted that the pandemic posed a "grave health threat" to Indigenous peoples around the world. These communities already have less access to basic services such as clean water and medical facilities. Diné Bikéyah, or the Navajo Nation, recorded a per person infection rate that was greater than every state by May 2020. There are fewer nurses and doctors serving the Navajo Nation. About 30 percent of homes on Nation territory do not have running water. This made it difficult to continually wash hands with soap and water. Diné Bikéyah leaders worked hard to lower infection rates and protect the elderly and those more vulnerable to COVID-19. They established curfews and social distancing.

During the first wave of the pandemic, many isolated Indigenous communities in Canada set up check points to limit access to prevent the spread. This community border control effort resulted in infection rates that were less than one-quarter than that of non-Indigenous Canadians. During the second wave, the more contagious variants were reported in several **reserves**. In some, the army was brought in to help with health care.

The government of Canada prioritized Indigenous peoples to be among the first to receive vaccines. In Indigenous communities, however, there is a history of distrust of government vaccines. To help reassure people that vaccines are safe, Indigenous nurses and doctors administered vaccines in some communities.

Chapter 3

Care Home Deaths

Long-term care (LTC) homes where elderly and disabled people live and are taken care of experienced higher infection and death rates from COVID-19. In the first wave of the pandemic, for example, 42 percent of deaths in America were in homes and facilities for the elderly.

In Canada, the infection and death rates in LTC homes were alarming. In April 2020, the army was called in to assist in homes in Quebec. LTC home deaths were 80 percent of Canada's COVID-19 deaths in the first wave (January 2020 to June 2020). The deaths were due to **understaffing**, overcrowding, and poor **infection control**. Those issues existed before, but they cost many lives during the pandemic. LTC home outbreaks continued in the second wave but tapered off during the third wave. By then, governments had prioritized vaccinations in LTC homes and that strategy helped to save lives.

Homelessness and COVID

When the pandemic started, experts warned that it could tear through homeless communities. In the United States, it isn't known how many homeless people have become sick or died from COVID-19. That's partly because homeless shelters were not asked by the government to keep records on infections or deaths.

Each state dealt with its homeless population differently during the pandemic. Connecticut reduced the number of people that could be housed in shelters. That helped keep them farther apart to prevent transmission. The state also moved homeless people aged 60 or older into hotels and placed testing facilities nearby. These actions helped lower infection rates.

> LTC homes were closed to visitors for months. That kept some residents safer from COVID-19. However, it cut them off from family and friends and made them very lonely.

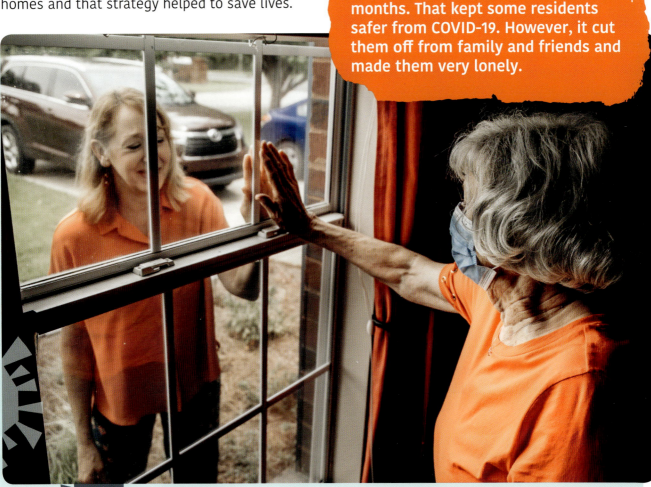

THE BATTLE FOR LIVES

Many homeless people work in low-wage jobs where it is not easy to stay 6 feet (2 m) away from others. Some live in homeless shelters or camps where it is also difficult to socially distance.

PANDEMIC HERO

Sir Captain Tom Moore

It started out in April 2020 as a small bet. **World War II** veteran Captain Tom Moore aimed to raise £1,000 ($1,380 U.S.) for charities by walking 100 laps of his garden. By the time he finished, on his 100th birthday, donations had topped £33 million ($45.5 million U.S.). Shuffling slowly with the help of his walker, Moore had captured the hearts of his country and the world. He encouraged people to support hospitals during a time when staff were working so hard to help people with COVID-19. Captain Tom adopted the slogan "tomorrow will be a good day." It gave hope to people stuck at home in lockdown. He was even knighted and made a "Sir" by Queen Elizabeth II. Sadly, Sir Captain Tom died in February 2021 after contracting COVID-19.

Captain Tom wore his war medals as he was knighted by the Queen in an outdoor, socially distanced ceremony.

Chapter 4

Government Responses

About half of the world's population was under some form of lockdown by April 2020. That's almost 4 billion people in 90 countries who were asked by their governments to stay at home. Lockdowns and other measures created new challenges for governments. Those included how to keep economies running and helping businesses function. Another challenge was making sure people could pay for the things they need, such as food and shelter.

In many ways, governments were flying by the seat of their pants. New rules and orders were made almost daily to control the virus and keep people safe. Many people suddenly lost their jobs during lockdowns. That meant governments needed to act fast to help people and businesses out. On March 27, 2020, the U.S. government passed the Coronavirus Aid, Relief, and Economic Security Act, known as the CARES Act. It was aimed at **stimulating** the economy with $2.2 trillion in aid to Americans and American businesses. The act gave $300 billion in cash payments to American citizens. Most received $1,200 each. It also increased unemployment payments to people who lost their jobs, and created a paycheck-protection program.

The CARES Act gave billions in loans to businesses big and small. It also helped out state and local governments so they could continue providing services. In January 2021, the new U.S. government released a national strategy for COVID-19. New laws also gave more relief, including more money.

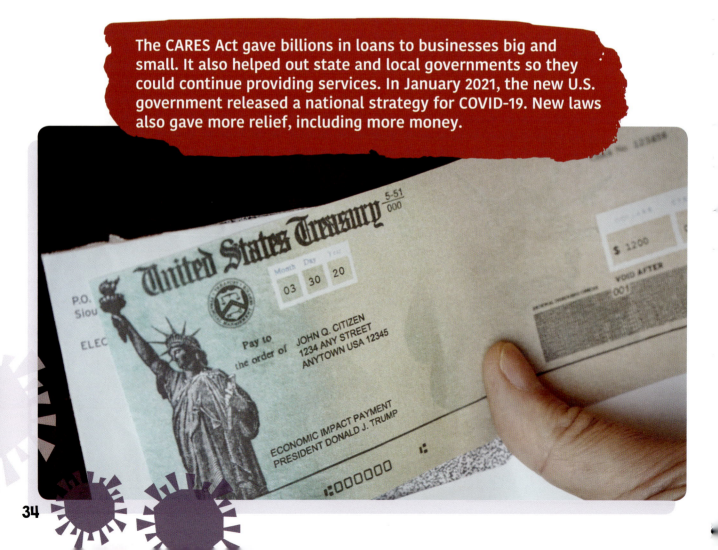

During COVID-19, people who could work from home were encouraged to do so. But not everyone had a job that could be done at home. Without government supports, more businesses would have failed and people would not have been able to pay for housing or food.

Supporting Citizens

Similar government support programs were set up by wealthier countries all over the world. Some were generous. Denmark supported workers up to 75 percent of their previous wage, with a maximum of 26,000 kroner ($4,229 U.S.) per month ending in January 2021. Canada announced an economic relief package on March 25, 2020. The Canada Emergency Response Benefit (CERB) provided $2,000 a month to people who lost jobs due to the pandemic, including self-employed people. It also provided support for businesses. An emergency wage **subsidy** was provided to keep people employed. That was combined with a number of other supports and loans to businesses and provincial governments. As a result, the Canadian government spent $240 billion in the first eight months of the pandemic.

Some countries, such as Sweden, did not lockdown in the pandemic's first wave. Swedes went to school and work, ate in restaurants, and did not wear masks in public. The strategy seemed to work at first, but by December 2020, infection and death numbers were climbing. Sweden had to change its pandemic plans.

Chapter 4

National Strategies

Handouts and economic stimulus packages were not the only way governments helped people. Most countries developed national strategies, or plans, for virus testing and vaccinations. They also planned how to buy and give out the supplies needed to fight the virus. When vaccinations became available, they were given first to those most at risk. That included the elderly, people with medical conditions, and **frontline** health care workers.

Country Vaccinations

Israel was one of the world leaders in fast COVID-19 vaccination rollouts. The tiny Middle Eastern country of 9.3 million people signed agreements to purchase a large number of vaccines from several different vaccine producers. This allowed Israel to start vaccinating on December 20, 2020. It vaccinated 8,000 people per day until a little more than half the country had the shot. By mid-February 2021, Israel reported a 94 percent drop in asymptomatic COVID-19 infections. That was among the 600,000 people who received two vaccine doses. This proved that widespread vaccinations worked to control the disease.

> Israel has a small population and size. It also has a history of planning for national emergencies. Both of these things helped it roll out vaccines quickly.

36

GOVERNMENT RESPONSES

Rollouts

The U.S. and the U.K. were also quick with their vaccine rollouts. By late January 2021, the U.S. was vaccinating nearly one million people per day. Canada, however, lagged far behind at first. This was despite having agreed to purchase more vaccines than any other country in the world. Unlike the U.S., U.K., India, and many other countries, Canada does not have a vaccine producer, or company that can make the vaccines in the country. It had to buy them from countries that do. Those countries gave vaccines to their citizens first.

Governments watched the numbers of infected. They declared states of emergency when needed, to protect citizens. A state of emergency is usually declared during disasters or wars. It allows the government more power to limit individual citizens' rights in order to keep everyone safe. In March 2020, 20 U.S. states declared a state of emergency for COVID-19.

Chapter 4

Vaccine Equality

Just 13 percent of the world's population got first pick on the vaccines. Those included the world's wealthiest countries—the 27 member countries of the European Union and five other rich nations. Together, they pre-ordered half of the world's vaccine supply. Middle-income and poorer countries had less access to vaccine supplies.

COVAX for the World

Early in the pandemic, the United Nations, the WHO, and other organizations set up a program called COVAX. It aimed to make sure low-and middle-income countries had access to vaccines. Some would be able to buy them, and others would get them as donations from wealthier countries and charities. COVAX was understood as helping the entire world. A majority of the world needed to be vaccinated.

If not, the virus would continue to mutate and the pandemic would never end.

The U.S. government's National Strategy for COVID-19 Response and Pandemic Preparedness is a large document on COVID-19 strategies. It was released in January 2021—a full year after the pandemic began. It noted that the country has to prepare for future outbreaks of COVID-19 in the U.S and throughout the world, even after an effective vaccine.

> Operation Warp Speed was a U.S. government strategy to manufacture COVID-19 vaccines as fast as possible. It was funded with $10 billion from the CARES Act. It helped get vaccines and treatments made.

GOVERNMENT RESPONSES

PANDEMIC HERO

Laurent Duvernay-Tardif missed the 2020 Superbowl with his team. He felt he was needed more in a long-term care home that had several outbreaks of COVID-19.

Laurent Duvernay-Tardif

He went from supporting teammates in a Superbowl championship to supporting seniors fighting COVID-19 in a long-term care home. Doctor and professional football player Laurent Duvernay-Tardif played for the Kansas City Chiefs in the 2019 National Football League Superbowl game. He chose not to play in the 2020 season. Instead, he worked in a long-term care home near Montreal, Canada, where he grew up. In an interview with *TIME* magazine, Duvernay-Tardif said he was inspired by his fellow athletes who had stood up for causes they believed in, including racial equality. Their efforts are what pushed him to support his own cause of health and medicine on COVID's frontlines. At the home, Duvernay-Tardif worked long shifts with few breaks, like any other health care worker. Along with five other pro athletes honored for their activism, Duvernay-Tardiff was named a *Sports Illustrated* 2020 Sportsperson of the Year.

Chapter 5

Preparing for the Future

While countries all over the world were still battling the effects of the COVID-19 pandemic, the WHO was urging them to prepare for the next one. The WHO's key message was that governments must put money into long-term disaster planning.

Millions of people died from COVID-19. Many others suffered long-term effects that won't be fully understood for many years. Economies were severely challenged, jobs lost, and lives were forever changed. Science, medicine, and public health advice saved many lives. By examining how some countries dealt with COVID-19 successfully, scientists say we can learn more about what to do next time.

Strong Strategy

South Korea was hard-hit by COVID-19 in the early months of the pandemic. But the country did not order a full lockdown. Instead, it used testing, contact tracing, and isolation to keep the virus under control. Contact tracing involves finding and notifying everyone an infected person has had contact with. Many walk-in testing centers were also set up. People who tested positive were ordered to quarantine themselves. The government monitored them by calling them twice a day. The movements of infected people were tracked through their cell phones. These efforts helped the country avoid lockdowns for the first year. It wasn't until a fourth wave from a new variant began in the summer of 2021 that South Korea decided tight restrictions would also be needed.

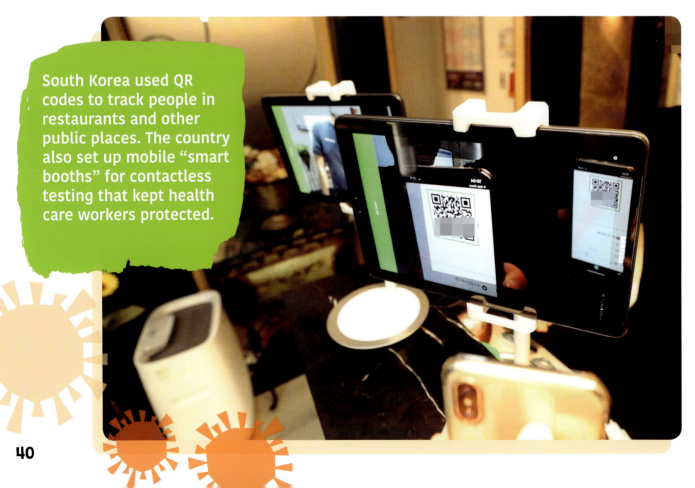

South Korea used QR codes to track people in restaurants and other public places. The country also set up mobile "smart booths" for contactless testing that kept health care workers protected.

In Africa, South Africa was hit the hardest by COVID-19. Its government put strict lockdown measures in place. It eased them in September 2020, when case counts went down. Then, a new faster-spreading variant of the virus appeared.

Neglect

In contrast to most of the world, a few countries took a lax approach. This led to deadly consequences. Brazil had one of the world's three highest case counts and deaths due to COVID-19. It had no official national strategy to fight the pandemic. In fact, for many months the government ignored precautions. This happened even while hospitals in some of the biggest cities were overwhelmed with sick and dying patients. This led to 12 million cases and 278,000 deaths in one year alone.

Collaboration Is Key

Many African countries were quick to use containment as a strategy. They worked together on plans to keep people safe. They also used the experience of earlier **Ebola** disease outbreaks in West Africa. The **African Union** (AU) wrote a joint African Continental Strategy on COVID-19. Early in the first wave of the pandemic, travel bans and quarantines for foreign travelers were established. Lockdowns were ordered by AU member countries that reported 100 cases. The Africa Centres for Disease Control (Africa CDC) monitored the disease. AU countries also combined resources to buy large amounts of PPE.

Chapter 5

Airline and tourism industries were devastated by the pandemic. Travel restrictions and health risks meant tourism dropped and fewer people flew. Many staff were laid off and airplanes sat unused at airports. For airlines, 2020 was the worst financial year on record.

Pandemics Affect Everyone

Pandemics are complex events because they affect billions of people in multiple ways. They have an impact even in places the virus didn't reach. The South Pacific islands of Tonga and Tokelau reported no COVID-19 cases in the first to third waves. But preventing the virus took a toll. Airports were closed and cruise ships were restricted. Their tourism-based economies suffered.

Green Zone Strategy

One coping strategy for future pandemics is called the Green Zone Strategy. It calls for governments to completely shut down virus spread early on. The idea is to stop the spread and lessen the overall impact on the economy. The Green Zone Strategy requires a strict, six-week or more shutdown everywhere in a country. All borders would be closed and travel would not be allowed. All events would be cancelled, and schools and businesses closed. Masks would be mandatory, and testing and tracing the disease would be a priority. The goal would be to get to zero transmission early in a pandemic. After zero transmission is achieved, areas would open up. Governments would continue to test, trace, and isolate those who test positive. This strategy is thought to be less harmful to businesses and schools than repeatedly opening and closing.
The Green Zone strategy was used with success in Taiwan, New Zealand, and Australia. Countries that managed to keep transmission rates low also fared better economically.

PREPARING FOR FUTURE PANDEMICS

Pandemic Prevention

Pandemics are not good for people or the global economy. Scientists are already working on preventing the next one. Proposals include programs to limit the spillover of animal diseases into human populations. Over the past 100 years, an estimated two animal viruses per year have adapted to infect humans. Programs that prevent buying and selling illegal wild meat could limit disease. Preventing deforestation can also help. When wild animal habitats are destroyed, animals move into human spaces. The edges of tropical forests are especially important, as this is where many animal-to-human transmissions occur.

Some scientists believe governments need to fund research on universal vaccines that cover all variants of a specific virus, such as the coronavirus. They argue this will help prevent future pandemics.

43

Bibliography

Intro

Farr, Christina, and Michelle Gao. "How Taiwan beat the coronavirus," CNBC, July 16, 2020.
https://www.cnbc.com/2020/07/15/how-taiwan-beat-the-coronavirus.html

Summers, Jennifer, Hsien-Ho Lin, Hao-Yuan Cheng, et al. "Potential lessons from the Taiwan and New Zealand health responses to the COVID-19 pandemic," The Lancet, October 21, 2020.
https://www.thelancet.com/journals/lanwpc/article/PIIS2666-6065(20)30044-4/fulltext

Chapter 1

Burki, Talha. "China's successful control of COVID-19," The Lancet, October 8, 2020. https://www.thelancet.com/journals/laninf/article/PIIS1473-3099(20)30800-8/fulltext

Cyranoski, David. "What China's coronavirus response can teach the rest of the world," Nature, March 17, 2020.
https://www.nature.com/articles/d41586-020-00741-x

"Naming the coronavirus disease (COVID-19) and the virus that causes it," World Health Organization.
https://www.who.int/emergencies/diseases/novel-coronavirus-2019/technical-guidance/naming-the-coronavirus-disease-(covid-2019)-and-the-virus-that-causes-it

Chapter 2

Ahmed, Issam. "Scientist's mRNA obsession once cost her a job, now it's key to COVID-19 vaccine," The Times of Israel, December 17, 2020.
https://www.timesofisrael.com/the-hungarian-immigrant-behindmessenger-rna-key-to-covid-19-vaccines/

Callaway, Ewen. "The race for coronavirus vaccines: a graphical guide," Nature, April 28, 2020.
https://www.nature.com/articles/d41586-020-01221-y

Hamblin, James. "The Coronavirus Is Evolving Before Our Eyes," The Atlantic, January 15, 2021.
https://www.theatlantic.com/health/archive/2021/01/coronavirusmutations-variants/617694/

Kalkman, Jori Pascal. "Military Crisis Responses to COVID-19," Journal of Contingencies and Crisis Management, September 27, 2020.
https://www.ncbi.nlm.nih.gov/pmc/articles/PMC7537208/

Liu, Yen-Chin, Rei-Lin Kuo, and Shin-Ru Shih. "COVID-19: The first documented coronavirus in history," Biomedical Journal, ScienceDirect, August 2020.
https://www.sciencedirect.com/science/article/pii/S2319417020300445

Neergaard, Lauran. "Years of research laid groundwork for speedy COVID-19 vaccines," PBS News Hour, December 7, 2020.
https://www.pbs.org/newshour/health/years-of-research-laidgroundwork-for-speedy-covid-19-vaccines

"Zhang Zhan: China jails citizen journalist for Wuhan reports," BBC News, December 28, 2020.
https://www.bbc.com/news/world-asia-china-55463241

Chapter 3

Abrams, Elissa M., and Stanley J. Szefler. "COVID-19 and the impact of social determinants of health," The Lancet, May 18, 2020.
https://www.thelancet.com/journals/lanres/article/PIIS2213-2600(20)30234-4/fulltext

Arnold, Carrie. "The US covid pandemic has a sinister shadow—drug overdoses," British Medical Journal, December 17, 2020.
https://www.bmj.com/content/371/bmj.m4751

"Pandemic meets Pandemic: Understanding the Impacts of COVID-19 on Gender-Based Violence Services and Survivors in Canada," Ending Violence Association of Canada, August 25, 2020.
https://endingviolencecanada.org/ending-violence-association-ofcanada-and-anaova-launch-report-on-findings-from-national-surveypandemic-meets-pandemic-understanding-the-impacts-of-covid-19-on-gender-based-violence-services-and-su/

Richardson, Lisa, and Allison Crawford. "How Indigenous Communities in Canada Organized an Exemplary Public Health Response to COVID," Scientific American, October 27, 2020.
https://www.scientificamerican.com/article/how-indigenouscommunities-in-canada-organized-an-exemplary-public-healthresponse-to-covid/

"Stigma and Prejudice," Centre for Addiction and Mental Health (CAMH).
https://www.camh.ca/en/health-info/mental-health-and-covid-19/stigma-and-prejudice

Sy, Stephanie, Lena I. Jackson, and Casey Kuhn. "Navajo Nation, hit hard by COVID-19, comes together to protect its most vulnerable," PBS News Hour, April 24, 2020.
https://www.pbs.org/newshour/show/navajo-nation-hit-hard-bycovid-19-comes-together-to-protect-its-most-vulnerable

Webster, Paul. "COVID-19 highlights Canada's care home crisis," The Lancet, January 16, 2021.
https://www.thelancet.com/journals/lancet/article/PIIS0140-6736(21)00083-0/fulltext

Zussman, Richard. "B.C. Reports Record Number of Illicit Drug Overdoses in 2020," Global News, February 11, 2021.
https://globalnews.ca/news/7634754/bc-overdose-numbers-2020/

Chapter 4

Bar-Yam, Yaneer. "Unsuccessful versus successful COVID strategies," New England Complex Systems Institute, December 13, 2020.
https://necsi.edu/unsuccessful-versus-successful-covid-strategies

"Coronavirus bailouts: which country had the most generous deal?" BBC News, May 8, 2020.
https://www.bbc.com/news/business-52450958

Mullard, Asher . "How COVID vaccines are being divvied up around the world," Nature, November 30, 2020.
https://www.nature.com/articles/d41586-020-03370-6

"Policy Responses to COVID-19," International Monetary Fund.
https://www.imf.org/en/Topics/imf-and-covid19/Policy-Responses-to-COVID-19#U

Chapter 5

Dobson, Andrew P., Stuart Pimm, Lee Hannah, et al. "Solutions for preventing the next pandemic," Harvard T.H. Chan School of Public Health, and C-Change Center for Climate, Health, and the Global Environment, July 24, 2020.
https://www.hsph.harvard.edu/c-change/news/preventingfuturepandemics/

Nikiforuk, Andrew. "Switch to a 'Green Zone' Strategy for Taming COVID-19," The Tyee, November 24, 2020.
https://thetyee.ca/Analysis/2020/11/24/Green-Zone-Strategy-Taming-COVID/

"The best time to prevent the next pandemic is now: countries join voices for better emergency preparedness," World Health Organization, October 1, 2020.
https://www.who.int/news/item/01-10-2020-the-best-time-toprevent-the-next-pandemic-is-now-countries-join-voices-for-betteremergency-preparedness

Timeline

Dec. 10, 2019 The first suspected novel coronavirus case emerges in China.

January 5, 2020 The WHO announces a pneumonia of unknown cause in Wuhan and advises against travel to China.

January 18, 2020 U.S. president Donald Trump is informed the virus is a serious threat. Cases are detected in Thailand, Japan, and South Korea, as well.

January 21, 2020 The United States confirms its first case of COVID-19.

January 28, 2020 China locks down Wuhan, with the entire Hubei province to follow on January 30.

January 31, 2020 A public health emergency is declared in the United States and all flights from China are directed to specific airports. A series of travel restrictions begins.

March 9, 2020 Italy records more than 1,000 cases per day. Canada announces its first COVID-19 death—a man in a British Columbia nursing home.

March 13, 2020 U.S. president Donald Trump declares a state of National Emergency.

March 16, 2020 China closes the 16 temporary hospitals it built to care for sick people. Europe records its first COVID-19 death.

June 11, 2020 Biotechnology company Moderna announces the final stage of trials for its coronavirus vaccine.

Fall 2020 New COVID-19 variants reported in the U.K., Brazil, and South Africa.

December 8, 2020 Britain administers world's first COVID vaccine shot.

December 12, 2020 U.S. COVID-19 vaccine rollout announced as country passes 300,000 deaths and 15 million cases.

December 14, 2020 First COVID-19 vaccine shot administered in Canada.

January 21, 2021 The U.S. releases its first National Strategy for COVID-19 and Pandemic Response.

June 10, 2021 With 64 percent of Americans having at least one shot of the COVID-19 vaccine, the U.S. unveils a plan to donate 500 million Pfizer COVID-19 vaccines to poorer countries. This will help ensure the world has access to COVID-19 vaccines.

Learning More

Books

Dobson, Mary. *Disease: The Extraordinary Stories Behind History's Deadliest Killers*. Quercus, 2008.

O'Brien, Cynthia. *The War Against COVID-19*. Crabtree Publishing, 2021.

Spilsbury, Louise. *The War Against Smallpox*. Crabtree Publishing, 2021.

Websites

https://www.cincinnatichildrens.org/patients/coronavirus-information/videos-for-kids-parents

The Cincinnati Children's Hospital has a page of videos and resources for kids, parents, and caregivers on understanding COVID-19.

https://kidshealth.org/en/parents/coronavirus-landing-page.html?WT.ac=p-ra

KidsHealth.org has information for adults and children on everything from social distancing to calming COVID-19 anxiety.

https://www.who.int/emergencies/diseases/novel-coronavirus-2019/interactive-timeline

The World Health Organization has an interactive timeline on the WHO's COVID-19 response. Readers can see how the virus and disease spread and what actions were taken.

Glossary

African Union A union of 55 African states

agency An organization

battlefield medicine The treatment of wounded soldiers near an area of combat that requires fast action and the adoption of new techniques to save lives

best practices A set of guidelines or rules that are the most efficient course of action in a specific situation

bias Prejudice in favor of or against something

biochemist A scientist who studies the chemical and physical actions of living things

cells The building blocks or smallest units of life

collaboration Working together to produce something

communist A political belief or government in which all property is publicly owned

discriminate To unfairly treat someone differently

Ebola A rare and deadly infectious disease that originated in sub-Saharan Africa

economy The wealth and resources of a country or geographic area

Glossary

epidemic A disease that is widespread in a community, population, or region

epidemiologist A scientist or doctor who studies outbreaks of diseases

ethnicity Belonging to a specific cultural or racial group

field hospitals Temporary hospitals usually set up during war or an outbreak of a disease

first wave The first mass groups to contract the virus

genetic structure The pattern or makeup that contains information about a living thing

H1N1 A novel, or new to humans, flu virus that spread to more than 200 countries in 2009, and caused 12,469 deaths

hereditary Inherited, or passed down, from ancestors

immunity Resistance to or protection from a disease

infection control Cleaning and procedures meant to keep a disease from spreading

innovations New methods or ideas

isolating Keeping someone apart from others

lockdown Closing down and restricting movement

medical journal A scientific journal that gives information to doctors about research

personal protective equipment Equipment such as masks and gloves worn by health care workers

press conferences News conferences in which officials talk to journalists

proteins Molecules in the body that do most of the work in cells, regulating the body's tissues and organs

provoking Deliberately trying to cause an outcome or emotion

public health The branch of medicine that deals with the health of a population

quarantine A period of isolation

quarrels Angry disagreements or arguments

reserves Areas of land set aside for the exclusive use of specific Indigenous peoples

respiratory Relating to breathing

SARS pandemic An outbreak of Severe Acute Respiratory Syndrome, a coronavirus that spread around the world in 2003

screening Testing people for a virus

second wave A high infection rate that came after the first wave

statistics Numbers that are collected to give information on something

stereotypes Oversimplified or untrue beliefs about specific groups of people

stimulating Encouraging

subsidy A sum of money given by the government to assist an industry

tracing Keeping track of

transmission Spread from person to person

understaffing Too few people at a job

World Economic Forum (WEF) A non-governmental organization that works to improve the state of the world through business, government, or academic study

World Health Organization (WHO) An agency of the United Nations that deals with international public health issues

World War II A global war (1939-1945) that involved most of the world

Index

Africa and South Africa 19, 41, 45
animal-to-human transmission 7, 9, 43
asymptomatic people 8, 36
at-risk populations 30–31
Australia 8, 42

battlefield medicine 16
Brazil 19, 41, 45
business closures 4, 29, 34–35, 42

Canada 22, 25, 26, 27, 29, 31, 32, 35, 37, 39
Centers for Disease Control and Prevention (CDC) 22, 25, 26
China 4, 6, 7, 8, 9, 10, 11, 18, 23, 25
contact tracing 4, 40, 42
containing the virus 28, 40, 41
COVAX 38
curfews 29, 31

deaths 4, 6, 9, 10, 17, 18, 24, 25, 26, 28, 30, 32, 33, 35, 40, 41, 45
Denmark 35
discrimination 25
distrust 24, 31
domestic violence and abuse 27
drug use and overdoses 25, 26
Duvernay-Tardif, Laurent 39

economic relief programs 34–35
effects 16, 40
Europe 35, 38, 45

Green Zone Strategy 42

H1N1 virus 9
handwashing 10, 20, 31
health care workers 18, 25, 36, 39, 47
homeless people 32, 33
hospitals 4, 6, 7, 10, 11, 16–18, 19, 23, 29, 33, 41, 45

immunity 8, 12, 14, 15
Indigenous peoples 30, 31

infodemic 24
isolation 4, 7, 10, 19, 25, 30, 40, 42
Israel 36
Italy 12, 18, 45

job losses 4, 34, 35, 40

Karikó, Dr. Katalin 15

Li Wenliang, Dr. 6
lockdowns 7, 10, 29, 33, 34, 35, 40, 41
long-term care homes 32, 39

masks 4, 10, 18, 20, 21, 22, 24, 29, 30, 34, 35, 42
mental health issues 25–26
MERS (Middle East respiratory syndrome) 12
messenger ribonucleic acid (mRNA) 14, 15
misinformation 24–25
monitoring 8, 29, 40, 41
Moore, Sir Captain Tom 33
mumps vaccine 14

"new normal" 23

Operation Warp Speed 38

pandemic status 9
personal protective equipment (PPE) 4, 18, 41
physical/social distancing 22, 23, 24, 26, 31, 33
protests 24
public health officials 10, 20, 21, 22, 24, 40

quarantine 23, 40, 41, 45

rights, limiting 37
routines, disruption of 25, 26
rumors 4, 6, 25

SARS 4, 12, 47
school closures 29, 35, 42
science and scientists 4, 6, 7, 8, 12–19, 21, 22, 24, 25, 28, 40, 43
sequencing 7, 12, 13
severe acute respiratory syndrome coronavirus 2 (SARS-CoV-2) 7, 12, 13, 18
smallpox 31
social media 4, 24
South Korea 40, 45
Spanish flu/1918–1919 flu pandemic 10, 28
spread 6, 7, 8, 9, 10, 14, 16, 17, 18, 22, 23, 28, 29, 31, 41, 42
states of emergency 8, 28, 37, 45
stay-at-home orders 7, 20, 27, 29, 33, 34, 45
stigma 25
Sweden 35
symptoms 6, 8, 16

Taiwan 4, 5, 42
testing 6, 8, 10, 23, 36, 40, 42
tourism economies 42
transmission 7, 18, 21, 32, 42, 43
travel restrictions 4, 7, 8, 10, 41, 42, 45
treatments 12, 13–14, 15, 16–17, 19, 25, 38

United Kingdom (UK) 13, 19, 29, 37

vaccines/vaccinations 12–15, 19, 24, 31, 32, 36, 37–38, 43, 45
Van Kerkhove, Dr. Maria DeJoseph 23
variants 18, 19, 31, 41, 43, 45
violence and abuse 27

World Health Organization (WHO) 7, 8, 9, 23, 38, 40, 45
Wuhan, China 4, 6, 7, 10, 11, 25, 45

Zhang Zhan 11

About the Author

Ellen Rodger is the author of dozens of books for children. Her grandmother was inspired to become a nurse after World War I and the 1918-1920 flu pandemic. She remembers her stories about nursing and her strict rules on cleaning and disinfecting.